This Book Belongs to

© 2018 All rights Reserved

www.ingramcontent.com/pod-product-compliance
Lightning Source LLC
Chambersburg PA
CBHW080423240526
45472CB00022B/2232